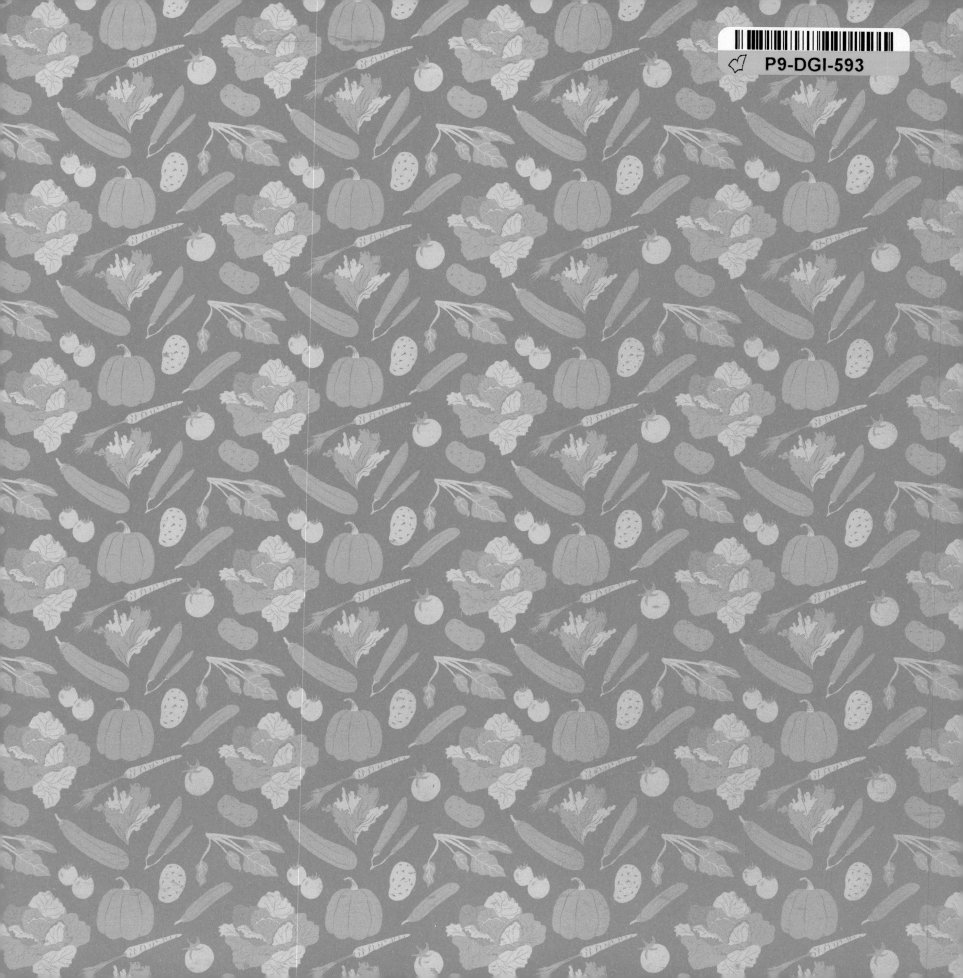

SECRETS
OF THE
VEGETABLE
GARDEN

Carron Brown

Illustrated by Giordano Poloni

Kane Miller
A DIVISION OF EDC PUBLISHING

A vegetable garden grows under the sun.

If you look closely between the stalks,
beneath the leaves, and in the soil, you
will see the animals and plants living there.

Shine a flashlight behind the page, or hold
it to the light to reveal what is hidden
in and around the vegetable garden.
Discover a small world of great surprises.

The seed of a tomato plant has been
sown in soil in a pot. When it has grown into
a seedling, it will be planted outside.

What three things does the seed need to grow?

Splish!

Splash!

Splosh!

The seed needs water,
warmth, and soil to grow.

Squawk!

Birds eating seeds planted in the garden take to the air.

Why are they flying away?

A scarecrow stands
tall in the garden.

It looks like a person,
which scares the birds
away from the seeds.

Flap!

Flap!

The tomato plant's roots grow strong under the soil.

Which creatures are in the soil?

Worms break down leaves and pieces of dead plants.

This makes food for growing plants.

Wriggle!

Rabbits like to eat the weeds that grow in the garden.

The gardener pulls the weeds out because the vegetables need space to grow.

Can you see the gardener's tools?

Creak!

The gardener keeps tools in the shed.

There's a spade for digging, a trowel for planting, a watering can for watering, and a rake for smoothing soil.

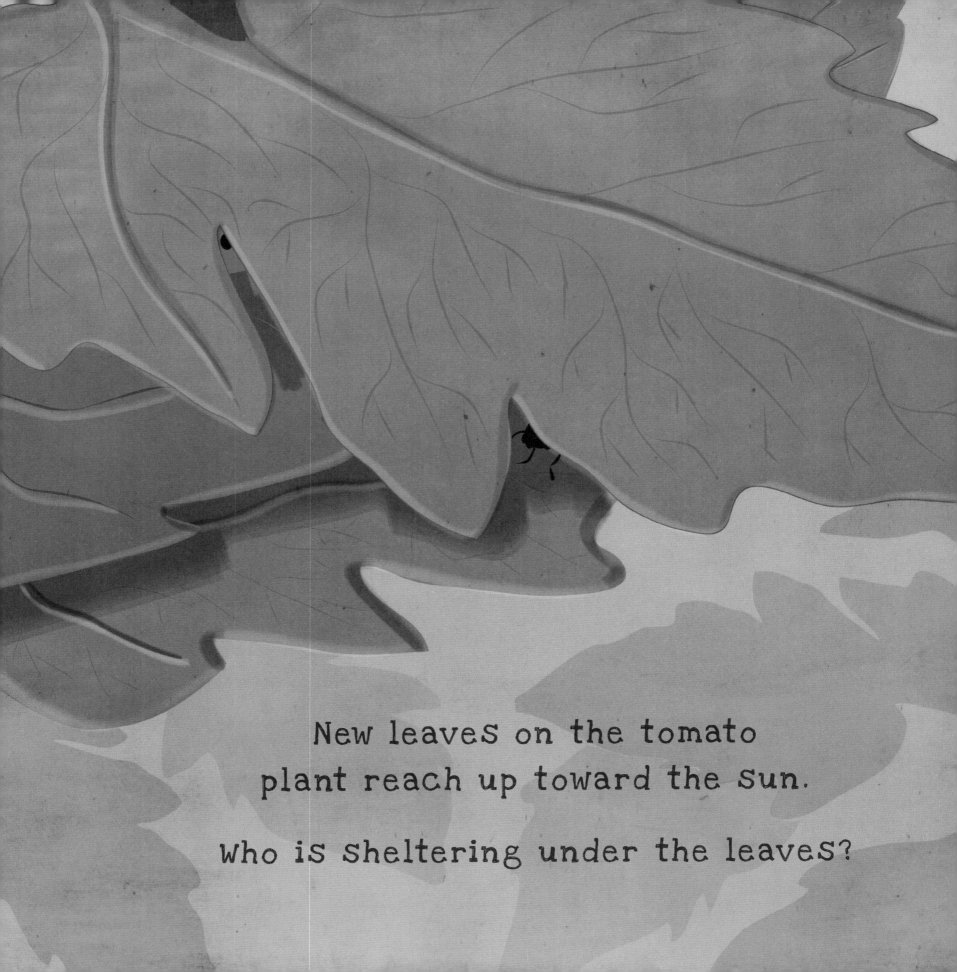

New leaves on the tomato
plant reach up toward the sun.

Who is sheltering under the leaves?

whirr!

Two ladybugs
have flown to
the green leaves.

They are spotted
beetles with wings.

Silky threads catch the light.

Who could have made this web?

Spin!

Spin!

Spin!

A spider
pulls silk from
inside her body
to weave a web.

The silk is sticky
and strong to catch
insects for her dinner.

The pitter-patter of rain falls on the soil and plants, helping them to grow.

Which animals feed in the rain?

Snails and slugs come out in the rain.
They eat the leafy vegetables.

Slither!

Gardeners do not like animals eating the vegetables. They can protect the plants with special sprays or nets.

What's inside this cloche?

It's lettuce!
The gardener
has covered it
to protect it
from slugs
and snails.

Tap!
Tap!

Small insects called aphids
like to eat the juicy leaves.

But another animal
likes to eat the aphids.

Can you see what it is?

Rustle!

Birds like this thrush peck
insects off the plants.

The tomato plant has grown flowers.

Bees carry pollen from one flower to another. This helps the tomatoes grow.

Where is the pollen?

A bumblebee picks up sticky
pollen on its furry body.

It visits the sweet-smelling
flowers to sip nectar.

Buzz!

This plant is growing tall.
Its tendrils twist around the trellis.

What is growing
in the pods?

There are peas growing in the pods.

Pop!

Green tomatoes are growing
where the flowers once were.
The leafy plants nearby are
also growing vegetables.

Can you see where they are?

Potatoes and carrots grow
under the ground.

Dig!

Dig!

Pumpkins and zucchini grow above the soil.

Who is nibbling
a pumpkin leaf?

A mouse is snacking
on a tasty leaf. Small
animals find plenty
to eat in a fruit and
vegetable garden.

Squeak!

The vegetables and fruit are being harvested.

Can you see what's in the wheelbarrow?

There are tomatoes, carrots, potatoes, cabbages, zucchini, and a pumpkin.

Yum!

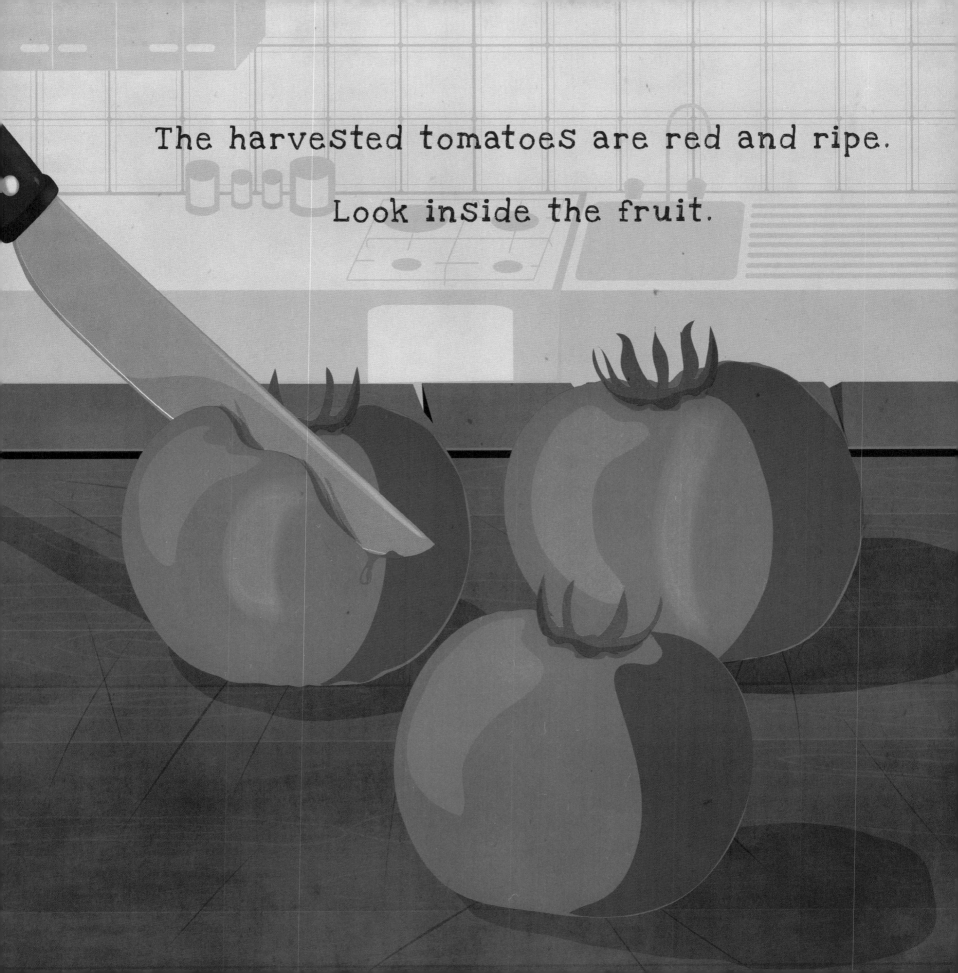

The harvested tomatoes are red and ripe.

Look inside the fruit.

The tomato is full of seeds. Each
seed can grow a new tomato plant.

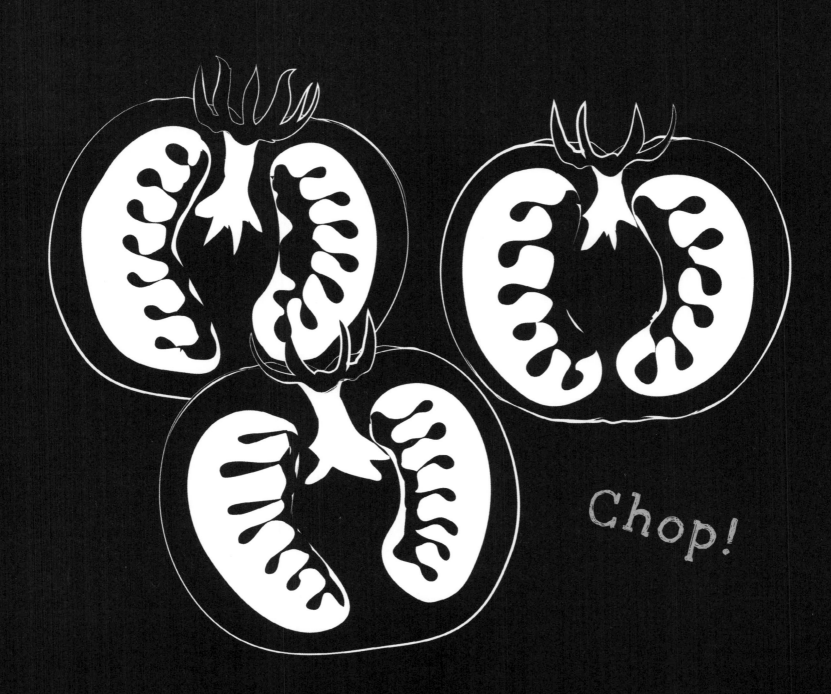

Chop!

Some tomato seeds are saved so they can become new plants. The rest of the tomatoes are chopped into a salad with some lettuce.

The vegetable garden will grow until fall. In spring, it will be time to sow seeds again.

There's more...

Now, look a little closer at the vegetables and fruits growing in the garden. See how they have different parts that change as they grow.

Seed A seed comes from the flower of a plant. If it has soil, heat from the sun, and water from rain or a watering can, it will grow into a new plant.

Roots A plant has roots that grow down into the soil. Roots take in water and food from the soil. The roots spread out and hold the plant in place.

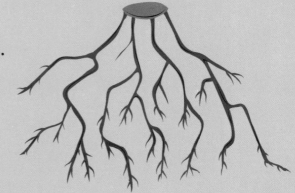

Stem The stem grows up from the roots and is at the center of the plant. It works like a straw, sucking up water and food to flowers, fruit, and leaves.

Leaf A leaf is flat to catch as much sunlight as possible. Food for the plant is made inside a leaf, using water, sunshine, and food from the soil.

Flower A flower is brightly colored and has sweet nectar to attract animals. Parts of a flower can make a seed if an animal brings it pollen from another flower.

Nectar Flowers make a sugary liquid called nectar. Animals such as birds, insects, and bats drink nectar. Bees use nectar to make honey.

Pollen A yellow powder called pollen sticks to a feeding animal in a flower. When the animal visits another flower, the pollen rubs off and this makes seeds in that flower.

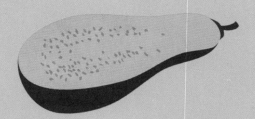

Fruit In some plants, fruit grows from the flower. Inside the fruit are the seeds, from which a new plant can grow. Tomatoes and eggplant are both fruits.

First American Edition 2016
Kane Miller, A Division of EDC Publishing

Copyright © 2017 Quarto Publishing plc

For information contact:
Kane Miller, A Division of EDC Publishing
PO Box 470663
Tulsa, OK 74147-0663
www.kanemiller.com
www.edcpub.com
www.usbornebooksandmore.com

Library of Congress Control Number: 2015938836

Printed in China

ISBN: 978-1-61067-413-3